The Big Helicopter

Story by Annette Smith

Illustrations by Naomi C. Lewis

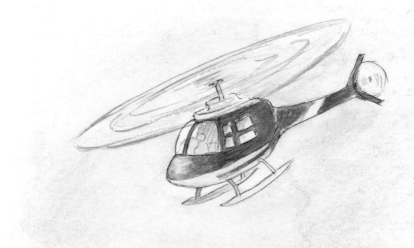

Matthew and Emma and Dad
went to see a helicopter.

Whirr, whirr, whirr!

Matthew looked up.
"I can see the helicopter,"
he shouted.

"Can you see it, Emma?"
said Dad.
"It looks little, up in the sky."

"Here it comes!" said Emma.
"The helicopter is coming down.
Come on. Run!"

"Run, Dad!" shouted Matthew.

They ran to see the helicopter.

Helicopter
Today at
2 o'clock

Whirr, whirr, whirr!

"Oh, no!" said Emma.

"The helicopter is going up.

Look at it!"

"It is going away,"
said Matthew.

"The helicopter will not come back," said Dad. "We will go home."

Whirr, whirr, whirr!

"Look!" shouted Emma.

"The helicopter is coming back.

I can see it!"

Helicopter
Today at
2 o'clock

Whirr, whirr, whirr!

The helicopter came down on the grass.

"The helicopter looks **big** down here," said Matthew.